IMAGES OF SCOTLAND

GLASGOW WEST

IMAGES OF SCOTLAND

GLASGOW WEST

PETER STEWART

TEMPUS

Frontispiece: St Mary's Cathedral in Great Western Road, 1930s.

First published 2005

Tempus Publishing Limited
The Mill, Brimscombe Port,
Stroud, Gloucestershire, GL5 2QG
www.tempus-publishing.com

British Library Cataloguing in Publication Data.
A catalogue record for this book is available from the British Library.

ISBN 0 7524 3658 9

Typesetting and origination by Tempus Publishing Limited.
Printed in Great Britain.

Contents

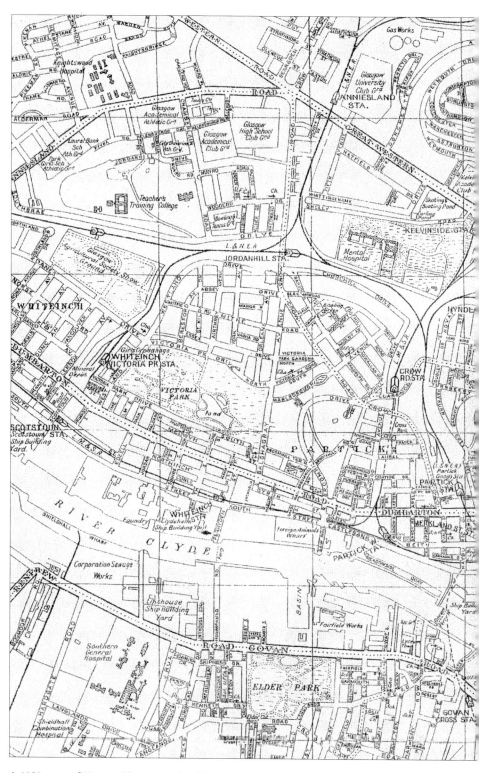

A 1930s map of Western Glasgow, north of the River Clyde, from the City to Knightswood.

Introduction

Over the centuries, the ancient town of Glasgow has expanded in all directions from the area around the Cathedral and the Molendinar river. By the late 1890s the centre had moved west and was now in George Square by the majestic Municipal Buildings, Walter Scott looking over it from a height. From the boundary by the River Kelvin, Partick and the Burgh of Hillhead were annexed in 1912 and 1891 respectively. By then, with continual development, Glasgow was confirmed as the Second City of the Empire.

The ancient Dumbarton Road by the Clyde ran westwards in Partick, while Great Western Road, a far-seeing inspiration planned as early as 1830, was laid from St George's Cross as far as Anniesland. Soon, by the second half of the century, magnificent mansions, flats and houses began to give the West End the solid and dignified feeling appreciated ever since. The continued growth in and around the area, with varying design, not all appreciated, has failed to spoil the general appearance of the West. The area between Kelvin Bridge and Anniesland, (W2, but now G12, felt by some a less distinguished postcode) was long regarded as the place to be, with its own unique accent. With well known schools, the Glasgow University and for years the BBC within the area, it always attracted residents and business. Things come and go, but the West End will remain a busy and very attractive place. Meanwhile, Partick W1 found itself G11.

After the First World War, Partick and West End further developed with modern housing, shops and businesses. Private cars were still a minority, even in the West End, and the trams and the ever improving buses in the '30s gave very efficient public transport, competing well with steam trains blowing their smoke underground and into the carriages. In the '50s it was still the tram and buses for all on their way down town. Electric trains did not appear until the 1960s after the trams had rattled off into museums and memory.

Where Dumbarton Road crosses the Kelvin, is the old Partick boundary, an area with a history going back to the twelfth century ('Perdeyk' or 'Perdyek'). Most of the old village was demolished for the railways and much of that has gone for the Clydeside Expressway linking the Clyde Tunnel and Kingston Bridge. The old road, though, is still congested at times.

Between the wars the ageing flats, black from years of smoke, suffered also from neglect. Restoration was impractical until the 1970s, after which control of rents was largely lifted and long-needed repairs began. Black dirt from a century of coal fires began to be removed transforming the streets and old flats. Such novelties as baths, personal lavatories and modern electricity became the norm. Knightswood's modern housing before the Second World War and ambitious building in Drumchapel after, gave families from smoky old city flats a move, along Great Western Road, to new planned communities with flats or houses and clean air.

The city's electric trams were part of the town, in and around Glasgow, from the start of the century until they finished their life in the 1960s. The unique colours, used to denote their routes, were still referred to long after numbers were allocated to them. The system was for years afterwards recalled wistfully by Glaswegians who had expected that the demise of the trams would speed the roads for the motor cars, the buses and the trucks.

Abbreviation: PPC – Picture Post Card

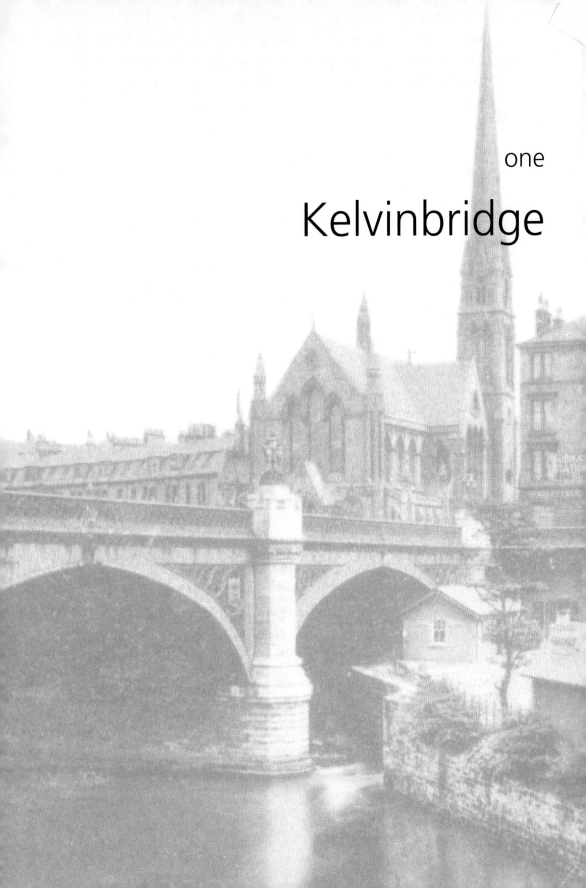

one

Kelvinbridge

Great Western Road begins at St George's Cross, seen in the far distance here beyond the two churches. The furthest tower is that of the Scottish Episcopal, St Mary's Cathedral. Trees conceal the River Kelvin which a hundred years ago marked the boundary with the Burgh of Hillhead. This view was taken in 1963, three years after the trams had disappeared. The closer Lansdowne Church is opposite Park Road. (PPC: Valentine, D8479)

The West End, seen across the Kelvin in 1937, with North Woodside Road on the right, opposite the entry to Kelvinbridge Subway. The lift down was closed forever when the Second World War started and steps, and later a moving lift, remained the only way down. The LMS railway station was down the small lane on the far left side of the river. An underground line to Maryhill survived into the 1960s. (PPC: Valentine A5911)

Kelvinbridge a century ago and nothing seen behind it seems different today. Railway land and coaches and trucks can just be seen. Kelvinbridge station (then Caledonian Railway) and the area around it is now mostly a car park. Stairs from the bridge, by the high building, descend to South Woodside Road and the entry to the Subway. 'Upholster, Art and Furniture' reads the advertisement at the Warehouse on the first floor of the building, while a 'Bedding Manufacturer' is advertised lower down. (PPC: Caledonia Series 532)

The Kelvin, by North Woodside Road, c. 1910. This was the boundary with the Burgh of Hillhead. The Glasgow Coat of Arms on the bridge is still duplicated by the Burgh's design. Glasgow Academy, seen in the background, has a history going back to 1847 in Renfield Street but today's school has long been in Colebrook Street.

Belmont Street, Looking North, Glasgow

Belmont Street, off Great Western Road, 1925. This street crosses the Kelvin by the church on the far side. Flats and houses on both sides have recently been replaced with modern residences, well built and not clashing with the older appearance of the street. The trees conceal Belmont Crescent. In the distance the street meets Wilton Street beyond which Maryhill Road is reached by North Kelvinside. (PPC: Raphael Tuck)

Stevenson Memorial Church, beside the river, seen here in 1905, dates from 1902, and was the church of the 1st Glasgow Company of the Boys' Brigade. The Boys' Brigade was started locally in 1883 by Sir William Smith, who came from a family of long military service, and it spread widely throughout the country. La Crosse Terrace is on the left before the river and a memorial is seen on the corner. As elsewhere, this entire road is now lined with cars.

GREAT WESTERN ROAD, GLASGOW

Above and below: The tall building on the left, Cooper & Co. (Liverpool & Glasgow), has changed little externally since 1880, but is no longer the magnificent shop it was for buying virtually anything and everything needed to satisfy the appetite. Coopers had branches all around the city but the firm did not survive the arrival of supermarkets. Food, solid and liquid, enjoyed on the spot, later kept the door open. The golden painted 'COOPER' sign on the road, to the side of the shop in Bank Street, survives after a century or more despite the passing of some millions of pairs of feet over it. This view from the 1920s shows 'Practical Electricians' at the corner shop while 'Speirs & Frame, Sanitary Gas & Heating Engineers', advertise beyond, higher up on the side of the next building. Tram No. 219, has stopped to pick up some passengers. (PPC: F.J. Ferry)

Opposite above: 'Hubbard's Bakery – Situate Smith Street, Hillhead, Glasgow', was founded in nearby Partick but has now long gone, as also have the popular Walter Hubbard shops and cafes that were once around the city. Smith Street was renamed Otago Street in around 1920 when many street names changed to avoid duplication. This 1909 advertising postcard bears on the reverse an advertisement for 'Hubbard's Celebrated Rusks' and a message of thanks to a customer for ordering them.

Right: Bank Street, from Glasgow Street to Great Western Road by Cooper's, *c.* 1950. A dignified and quiet street, joining with University Avenue at Gibson Street, and home to a few small private hotels towards the main road. The change to one-way traffic has affected its peace somewhat. Neglect of buildings in wartime and afterwards made it untidy and somewhat grubby. More recently improvements to the buildings have restored much of the street's original appearance, though the row of busy small shops, as elsewhere, has reduced. Trees along the street have increased in size and number, lately, further changing its appearance. (M. Wild)

Right: Glasgow Street was so named when it was the way to the river before the Great Western Road was built. Hillhead High School, built in the 1930s for secondary pupils, is just visible on the left side of the street, before it ends at Hillhead Street in this view of 1937. Here as elsewhere in much of Kelvinside, these old houses and flats look little changed, except for the loss of the iron garden railings, taken away during the Second World War.

Opposite below: This art deco building from the 1920s still exists opposite Cooper's in Great Western Road and was a popular place for lunch for many, including students from the academy and the university. After Hubbard's it was owned by City Bakery which closed in 1970. The building is protected but the new occupants transformed the lower half when converting it for the present restaurant and that part is anything but art deco.

Great Western Road looking towards town, with South Park Avenue on the right. In the early 1900s tramwire posts could safely be erected in the centre of the road with virtually no traffic except horse-drawn vehicles. The buildings seen here are all recognisable today but cleaner than in those days of almost perpetual coal-burning fog.

A view down Great Western Road to Byres Road and the Botanic Gardens in 1923. The line of shops starts at Hillhead Street, descending to Cecil Street, while the line of houses on the other side of the road is on Ruskin Terrace. The nearest shop, the Northern Farmer's butchers shop, closed in 1969 after eighty years in business there. (Valentine)

This view looking towards Byres Road and the Botanic Gardens, with Buckingham Terrace on the right and the Kelvinside Parish Church on the left, is from the early 1900s. At Kersland Street an advertisement on John Campbell's shop is for W. & A. Gilbey, Wine Importers & Distillers, and a bank is next door. Apart from a couple of trams in the distance, all the vehicles are horse drawn, one delivering for Campbells. (PPC: Caledonia Series)

Thirty years on, this picture is much the same except for the change to motor transport, with buses joining the trams. Past the crossroads is Botanic Gardens station with its two white columns; competition from buses and trams closed it in the thirties. Queen Margaret Drive is on the right beyond the large, stately houses. A lady at the kerb is wielding a long stick for whatever reason we shall never know. (PPC: Valentine 215968)

Opposite: Kelvinside Parish (previously Free) Church at the Byres Road corner on the right, opposite Queen Margaret Bridge, 1930s. The lady is crossing the road towards Botanic Gardens station. The tram about to pass her is making for Kirklee, a short distance up Great Western Road. The church, opened in 1858 and closed around the end of the century to be converted into restaurants.

Below: Looking along Great Western Road towards town on the same afternoon as the scene opposite, with the station on the left behind the tram stop and the A82 road sign. The tram in the distance is passing the entrance to the Botanic Gardens at the corner of Queen Margaret Drive.

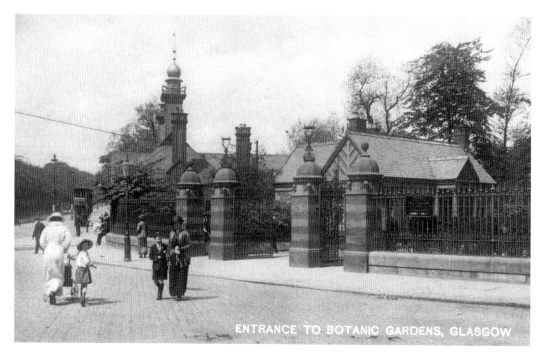

Above: The main entrance to the Botanic Gardens at the corner of Great Western Road and Queen Margaret Drive in the early 1920s. On the left, with the tower, is the Botanic Gardens station. Trains ran underground from the town on the way to Maryhill. Although the service continued the stations here and at Kirkhill were closed in the 1930s.

Right: Art on display in Queen Margaret Drive on a sunny summer afternoon in 1959. Note the dangling artistic hanger from the great 'T' attached to the railings of the Botanic Gardens. It almost reminded you of Paris. The annual summer celebration in the West End has since seen greater displays of local art.

Below: The 'Glasgow Girl Series' was drawn by A.G.A. and published by Millar & Lang in the early 1900s. It was a popular way to make humorous digs at city females. Hillhead was a favourite target because of its dialect but this description of their speech would not have amused the Hillhead Girl.

" Glasgow Girls " Series.

The Hillhead Girl.

Oh, coy and dainty little maid,
   My love for you is burning :
Alas! I cannot, dare not hope,
   For you that love returning.
I dream of you the whole day long,
   I dream of you in bed—
Oh, spurn me not, thou fairest flower,
   Sweet Maudie of Hillhead.

                    A. G. A.

HILLHEAD—Pronounced "Hillhed" or "Hullheed"—is situated upon the borders of Kelvinside and is therefore affected by the dialect peculiar to the latter district. It is chiefly inhabited by landladies and other land-sharks.

Opposite below: A comical dig at the Kelvinside 'ex-cent' illustrated in a postcard from 1903. The entrance to the Botanic Gardens was always a popular place for young couples to meet in the evening on the way to a dance, the cinema or any other pleasure, especially if the night was as dark as shown here - and no better place to get the tram into town and back home for a few pence. (PPC: F. Baumeister, signed A.G.A.)

QUEEN MARGARET BRIDGE, GLASGOW

W. RALSTON LTD.
GLASGOW

Queen Margaret Bridge replaced the old (Kelvin) Hamilton Drive around 1930. Kelvinside church is in the distance and the flag is flying on the BBC building. North Park House, on Kelvin's south banks, was given in 1894 by Mrs John Elder for Queen Margaret's College female students' medical department. In 1935 the college moved to the university and the buildings were sold to the BBC.

QUEEN MARGARET BRIDGE, GLASGOW

Beyond the bridge the Drive is now a major route to Maryhill Road towards Bilsland Drive. Past the bridge Kelvin Drive is on the left by the Botanic Gardens. Fergus Drive, across Queen Margaret Drive, rose sharply for a fine view until the road was filled with high built housing on the opposite side. An open-topped car, registration number XP 6759, with perhaps the owner beside it, and a group of schoolboys behind him. The pavements are quite busy, so possibly it was lunchtime when this scene was recorded in the 1930s.

Above: Queen Margaret's College gardens seen in the late nineteenth century, before female university students arrived. The old Queen Margaret Road Bridge to Hamilton Drive remained till 1970 for pedestrians. After its arrival in the 1930s the BBC expanded beyond much of Hamilton Drive but early in the present century was planning to move south across the Clyde.

Right: 'Auntie Kathleen', the well-loved children's broadcaster from Glasgow, who only retired from broadcasting in 1969. She began in the very different world of 1923 when she was known as 'Auntie Cyclone', before the BBC had been born. The 'Auntie' (originally 'Aunt') title was dropped forever in 1937. Her *Children's Hour*, regular for many years, was a most popular programme. Her natural soprano voice would fill in any gaps in the programme. Stories read in her *Hour* would be presented and dramatised by well-known personalities such as Gordon Jackson, Stanley Baxter and Tom Conti. Youngsters often contributed as actors in the plays. (Information given by Scottish BBC is gratefully acknowledged)

Before Queen Margaret Drive and the wide bridge over the Kelvin were built, the way across was by the old Queen Margaret Bridge, a short distance down the river (the Walker's Bridge) to Hamilton Drive. This remained until 1970. Left of the massive wall behind the bridge in this photograph of around 1905 are the steep 'Sixty Steps' rising to Wilton Street. (PPC: W. Ross)

Kelvin Drive, alongside the Botanic Gardens from Queen Margaret Drive to Clouston Street (right) and the Kirklee Bridge (left), c. 1955. In 1941 bombing destroyed a petrol station at the start of Wilton Street causing damage to several houses in Kelvin Drive. Only one car can be seen parked in the far distance but this view today would show cars parked night and day along each side of the road.

Kirklee Bridge crosses the Kelvin, opposite Clouston Street, to the wide Kirklee Road before it turns toward Great Western Road, 1905. This area contains many one hundred-year-old mansions with a mixture of other smaller and more modern houses scattered among them. Less than a mile behind the bridge can be seen the Maryhill Infantry Barracks, demolished after the Second World War but not before Hitler's Rudolf Hess had spent a night or two there. (PPC: Caledonia, Series 50)

Looking along the Kelvin between the trees from Queen Margaret Drive Bridge, the crossing over the river for those walking through the park. There is quite a climb up the other side through the trees to reach the greater part of the Botanic Gardens.

The Botanic Gardens, opened to the public in the 1890s and became a part of Glaswegian life for all ages. This is a view from the entrance to the Glass Houses in the 1950s. Keeping off this grass here is strictly enforced but there is plenty more elsewhere for energetic young ones. As well as walking and playing and sitting in the sun, it has always been a place for the study of plants, including tropical species and others linked with the university's interests.

Above: The Kibble (Art) Palace, seen here in 1939, was an attraction ever since it arrived from Coulport in 1873. Its plants, ponds, fountains and statues were admired from the start and musical soirées were enjoyed too. More recently it has attracted photographers taking marriage photographs. Rectoral addresses were delivered here by Disraeli and Gladstone. In the early twenty-first century the Kibble Palace was disassembled and taken away for much needed cleaning and rebuilding. (PPC: Valentine A8224)

Opposite below: Outside the Glass Houses in the 1920s. A young girl tries to drag her sister into the doorway, perhaps with an early interest in gardening, another couple of young ones watch, two ladies on a bench look on, a solitary man continues with his walk – the sort of scene that is as familiar here today as it has been for many years. (PPC: Caledonia)

Above: Summer 1957 at the Kibble Palace and children lean over to see the fish swimming around in the circular pond, an activity enjoyed and long remembered. For later generations a metal guard was added to the stone surround making it impossible to lean over the edge and fall in.

Peacefully wandering around the warm indoor plant houses was always a popular activity, especially on wet or chilly days. Fine days would see mothers and nurses sitting on the benches, out with their youngsters and babies. There is a good selection of prams and their occupants out on this day in the 1920s.

Above: A chilly winter's day in the Gardens but there are plenty of people of all ages out for a late afternoon walk. The church at Byres Road is on the right. Children are out in force with their mothers or nurses and the seats are filled from one end to the other. (PPC: Taylor's of Woodlands Road)

Opposite below: Grosvenor Terrace stretching west from Byres Road. Long closed, the station building survived until it was burnt down in 1971. More serious later was the fire destroying Grosvenor Terrace, across the road, including number one, the hotel, at the corner. Later restored, the original design was unchanged though rebuilt with different material. This scene in 1952 is of a morning almost free from vehicles, a personal new car being still hard to get at this time. (PPC: Valentine B5853)

The Kelvin Botanic Gardens, Glasgow

Above: The River Kelvin divides the Botanic Gardens as it flows under Kirklee Bridge. A steep walk down to the bridge across the water leads to the play area and the swings. Kirklee railway station, just out of sight above the bend in the river, was later replaced by a private house, finally making the line closed forever. (PPC: Taylor's of Woodlands Road)

GREAT WESTERN ROAD AND ENTRANCE TO BOTANIC GARDENS, GLASGOW   B 5853

Above: Looking west along Great Western Road in around 1902. One tram returning to Dennistoun passes another on the way to Kelvinside terminus. Walking along the pavements on the left after church on Sunday with your family was a popular activity in the early years of the twentieth century. (PPC: Misch & Co.)

Left: Belmont and Hillhead parish church on Observatory Road was opened in October 1876 and has been described as a Presbyterian copy of Saint Chapelle. In 1950 the congregation combined with Hillhead parish church which later closed. The front car has a Lanarkshire registration number and there is an Austin 30 further down the street.

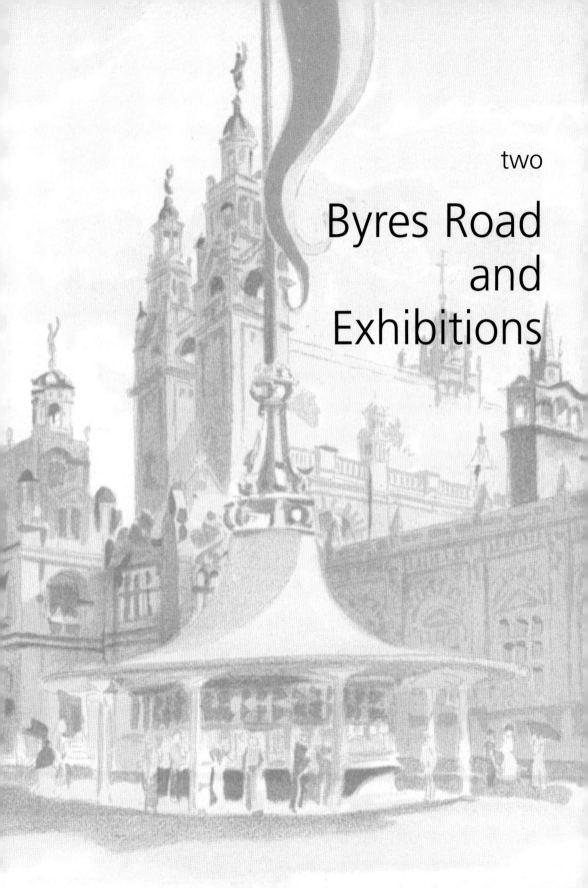

two

Byres Road and Exhibitions

Byres (or Byars) Road, the lower part of Victoria Street, around 1911, before Partick joined Glasgow. The top of the road originally curved to the right. A lone tram makes its way down road passing the Hillhead Subway. The shop facing sold saddles and harnesses. The left corner shop at Dowanside Road, with the blinds down, displays 'Victoria Cross', above the window and Stead & Simpson was the next door shop. (PPC: Valentine, 69789)

A rainy day on the same upper part of Byres Road in the 1990s. The last tram disappeared in the '60s but the street soon became congested with traffic for much of the day. The buildings here have hardly changed in appearance except for their much cleaner modern look. Few of these shops are now locally owned.

Right: A reconstruction of Govan Station at the Transport Museum, 1985. The Subway opened on 14 December 1896 and the city took over control of it in 1923. Electrification, not before time, was completed in December 1935 and it was re-named the Underground. An eastern circle, once proposed, was never pursued. The Victorian cars, with some improvements, survived until 1976 when the system was closed for refurbishment and two years later re-opened. The ancient trains were gone and the fifteen identical, unattractive stations were rebuilt to give the modern ones of today.

Below: The new 1980 train, nicknamed 'The Clockwork Orange', can be seen here at Buchanan Street. The twenty-first century has seen the Underground given back its original name, the Subway.

Vinicombe Street, off the top of Byers Road, was named, it was said, by the builder who came from a village of that name in Cornwall. This photograph of a short street rising to Kersland Street in 1937 shows house No. 6 advertising a seven-room flat for let. For many years after the war flats were never let empty, only furnished, as, once in you could not be put out. (JGS)

The Salon in Vinicombe Street opened as the Hillhead Picture Salon in 1913 and was a very high-class cinema with Art Nouveau panels and ornaments. At first the orchestra was led by the well-known Herr Wilhelm Iff, but during the war a black singer was a local sensation. There were tea and biscuits from silver trays. The Salon was slow to modernise in the twenties but survived in the century. (Bruce Peter)

Opposite below: F&F (Fyfe & Fyfe's) cinema was bought in 1922 by two brothers who provided roller skating, ballroom dancing and Sunday cafe concerts. It had previously been the Star Picture Palace and Theatre of Varieties which had been providing some films since 1919. In the days before sound arrived a versatile musician, usually a pianist, would skillfully follow the drama and play an accompaniment and also play between films. (Thanks for assistance and image to the SRA, The Mitchell Library Information Learning, Glasgow City Council)

Byres Road, Partick

Valentines Series

Above: A green tram, No. 555, built in 1901, bound for the Botanic Gardens, is seen passing Lawrence Street here in around 1905. Until 1937 the tram routes were recognised by the tram colours: green, blue, red, yellow and white. A top-hatted gentleman is driving a horse-drawn carriage in the centre of the road. To the right is University Avenue, some years ago turned halfway to connect with Highburgh Road. The lower half of the Avenue now has a great new medical building and car park. (PPC: Valentine)

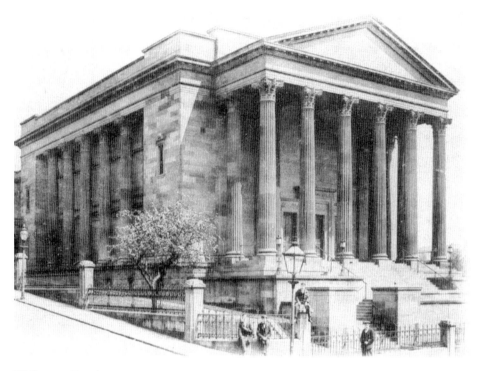

Wellington Church on University Avenue in 1902. The building dates from 1884 following the church's move from Wellington Street in the city centre. Its appearance today is unchanged after a century and it continues to serve the community. (PPC: F. Baumeister)

Glasgow and West of Scotland College of Domestic Science or 'Dough School' has been for some years a part of Glasgow University. This elegant building remains as seen here, but is now nearly surrounded by post-war additions. Some well-built residences in Eldon Street were demolished for the extension of the modern Domestic Science department. (PPC: Herald Series; A. Hardie, Woodlands Road)

The white tram, No. 742, has just set off from the university terminus en route to Pollokshields, *c.* 1904. For decades the white tram carried students to and from town and was the subject of a 1904 verse: A white car glides up from the sleeping town/ And from the east/ Where the fog, impotent, inert,/ Lolls in a yellow lump/ There twines the old, grey college/a long and sinuous line of hairy /hopeful freshmen. Swift be their passing!/Exams all vanquished, and their Arts course run/The grad. got over, and, near the gate,/Some white car waiting,/Let them be whirled far from the ken of profs/Far from the weary, winter session's grind. (PPC: Bell's Series, London)

Hillhead U.F. Church, opposite the Student Union, is now the university's Gilmorehill Halls, the Centre for Theatre, Film and Television Studies.

GLASGOW UNIVERSITY UNION.

Above: The present Student Union dates from 1931 and was for males only for many years. Two guineas a term for five consecutive years gave life membership, mostly to medics. Alcohol was unavailable except for dances and other important evenings such as the famous December Daft Friday; a night of dancing which ended with breakfast. Couples' wild and friendly celebrations went on up in the dark rooms and elsewhere.

Left: Glasgow University Chapel was built in memory of those from the university who died in the First World War. The chapel was erected in the late twenties under the lead of Principal McAlister and, in addition to the regular morning use, it has seen countless marriages. It was thought by some that the Principal might also have been equally keen to improve other aspects of the University progress.

Glasgow

Old Gateway at New College

Above and right: In 1870, Glasgow University moved from College Street, its ancient home, selling the land to the Glasgow & South Western Railway for building a goods station. Founded in 1451, the second oldest university in Scotland after St Andrew's, the old college buildings had known many famous students and professors. The front of the Old Gateway was moved from the old to its new home. Dating from the seventeenth century, with King Charles II's plaque in place, it has remained a useful entrance at the bottom of University Avenue. The move to the west was controversial, as was the choice of architect. It has often been mooted that had it been delayed perhaps Charles Rennie Mackintosh would have suggested something different – something very different. (PPC: Caledonian)

University Tower and West Wing, Glasgow.

Left: The University Tower and West Wing in the early 1900s. Sir George Gilbert Scott was responsible for the building, with some designs modified later by his two sons for buildings which had not been completed in 1870, largely due to financial difficulty. The steps were another transfer from the old college and are now seen beside the chapel.

Below: Extensions to the university buildings continued almost without stopping over the years as can be seen here in the 1920s. The entry gate, just on the left, past the Partick Bridge, is beside the wide walk into Kelvingrove Park. The park has a long history and was host to three major exhibitions for which in many ways it was a perfect site. (PPC: Taylor's, Woodlands Road)

Partick Entrance to University, Kelvingrove Park, Glasgow.

'Let us haste to Kelvin Grove, bonnie lassie, O!' A fine introduction to the 1901 International Exhibition in Kelvingrove Park, a great success following the popular 1900 Paris Exhibition. This humorous postcard shows an anxious couple making their way - anyone was welcome! (PPC: National Series, M. & L.)

Sandyford Street was the original name for Sauchiehall Street beyond Charing Cross. The main entrance of the Exhibition is shown on an 'Entirely Printed in Glasgow' set published by Bauermeister from an attractive alternative dozen by A.H. Scott. The equally good postcards were from the famous artist H. Cassiers from across the English Channel but an excessive quantity was ordered.

EXHIBITION ENTRANCE

Left: The opening of the twentieth century saw the city at the peak of its confidence. The 1888 Exhibition had helped to build the new Art Galleries and Museum and encouraged future achievements. Although the enjoyable variety of features at the Exhibition brought in the crowds, the industrial displays of the Grand Avenue and the Machinery Hall were more serious elements that showed the range and quality of Scottish industry and also that of other countries represented. (H. Cassiers)

Below: The Russian Section was one of seven foreign displays which also included France and Japan alongside those from the Dominions and Colonies of the day. 1901 was seen by many, following the unpleasant military shock of the Boer War, to be the start of a new and peaceful century which would see further growth of the Empire, with a trusted new King. Glasgow would remain the Second City. (PPC: Bauermeister)

GLASGOW EXHIBITION.
The Russian Section.

Opposite page: The River Kelvin running towards the Clyde was a source of popular recreation for the visitors, well shown in a set of comic postcards, anonymously drawn. The Canadian Water Chute was the most popular side-show, though it cost sixpence a thrill! An American miniature railway skirted the Russian section and a gondola was seen in the Kelvin. In the industrial years the Kelvin was hardly clean and by the time it reached the Clyde it was less than that, but even so it became the Venice water. Kelvingrove Park, with its convenient setting, its river and Cranston's Tea Rooms, seemed a perfect site for an Exhibition.

GLASGOW EXHIBITION. 1901.

GLASGOW EXHIBITION. 1901.

Above: The Concert Hall, with seats for 3,000, was built in a Venetian style but criticised because of an echo and also because of its programme, mostly of 'parochial' concerts. It did not attract the range of visitors that had been anticipated but it was nevertheless well attended by local citizens. (A.H. Scott)

Left: The new Art Galleries and Museum, opened in 1901, was closed for two years at the beginning of the twenty-first century to remove years of accumulated dirt, meanwhile taking the advantage to modernise without affecting the grand interior. It could now show the original magnificent sight not seen by anyone now alive. (A.H. Scott)

Opposite below: The Kelvin Grove Street entrance looks ready to welcome the Duke and Duchess when they arrive to open the Exhibition on 3 May but the sparse crowd outside suggests that this was a rehearsal before the day. Above the entrance the character of the exhibition is clearly laid out: 'National History, Art and Industry, Glasgow 1911', and the Scottish Royal Arms, *In Defens.*

Above: The year 1911 saw another major exhibition, the Scottish National Exhibition in Kelvingrove Park, but this had little in common with the 1901 Exhibition. This one dwelt on the theme of history and also was intended to be a 'one-up' on Edinburgh's exhibition of 1907. The Duke of Connaught opened the show on 3 May, which was unfortunately a rather wet one. His Majesty and the Queen were meanwhile opening the Festival of Empire at the Crystal Palace. The royal procession is seen here coming up Kelvingrove Street towards the entrance for the opening. (PPC: Rotary Photographical Series)

THE KELVIN GROVE STREET ENTRANCE.
THE SCOTTISH NATIONAL EXHIBITION, GLASGOW.

The opening ceremony procession reaches the Palace of History, driven in the local Argyll cars. As expected, the Palace had a huge collection of relics. The building was based on the Palace of Falkland – this time the exhibition was to be unmistakably Scottish. National pride had been awakened but upset also, to some extent, when King Edward's coronation gave him to be the Seventh of Great Britain. (PPC: Reliable Series)

The Fairy Fountain was in front of the Concert Hall in the square which included the Palace of Art. The Fountain was lit up at night, making the square a popular attraction. It was described as 'a veritable charm by night', using '300 gallons of water a minute, illuminated by 23,000 candle power'. (PPC: Rotary Photo)

Miss Cranston, most famous for her Tea Rooms and Dining Room in Glasgow and since remembered as the faithful client of Mackintosh, catered for the unlicensed White Cockade. The company had also catered in 1901 and many who remembered the earlier years were dismayed when the 1938 Exhibition, across the river, was served by a different caterer. It is not clear whether the Japanese Tea Gardens actually served Japanese tea.

An Tigh Osda – The Village Inn.

The Highland Village, 'An Clachan', was a popular attraction, though siting it close to the 'Arctic' and 'West African' villages, and the amusements, led some apparently to feel this implied it might be a backward or primitive part of the world. There was an admission fee and the Highland people there were all that the public expected. On the reverse side of this 'caird phostail' (postcard) one was informed that 'The visitor can be refreshed here with wholesome fare, served by fair maidens whose accents are those of the Hebrides'.

THE MYSTERIOUS RIVER.
THE SCOTTISH NATIONAL EXHIBITION, GLASGOW

Above: The Mysterious River was as popular as an exhibit as any though the couple on the front seat here don't look too comfortable. This Amusement was in the north area of the park. The Kelvin Way had not been completed, and the Scenic and Aerial Railways and some smaller attractions occupied the space from Park Terrace to the river and beyond.

THE MOUNTAIN RAILWAY
THE SCOTTISH NATIONAL EXHIBITION, GLASGOW.

THE WHIRLPOOL.
THE SCOTTISH NATIONAL EXHIBITION. GLASGOW.

Above: The Whirlpool. More people seem to be watching than whirling or queuing up at the entrance in front of the Carlton Restaurant. There are some safety life belts hanging around just in case of accidents. The cafe next to it is offering tea and iced fruit drinks. The Mountain Scenic Railway on the right advertises 'Patrons, the Royal Family'. They probably didn't try the Whirlpool! (PPC: Rotary)

Right: The Palace of Industry was the largest building in the Exhibition, though not regarded as the most important. On a part of the site occupied by the 1901 Hall of Industry, it attracted designers from Europe and Japan in addition to those from Britain. The public also found various domestic articles such as vacuum cleaners, ice cream freezers and other tempting wonders to be bought from their favourite shops.

Opposite below: The Mountain Railway was another sure favourite, though possibly the 'ups and downs' were not as hair-raising as are the 'upside downs' of the twenty-first century. Looking at the riders' expressions, no-one seems to be anything but happy. (PPC: Reliable Series)

· THE · HALL · OF · INDUSTRY ·
SCOTTISH · EXHIBITION ·
· NATIONAL HISTORY ·
· ART · & · INDUSTRY ·
· GLASGOW · 1911 ·

THE AERIAL RAILWAY.
THE SCOTTISH NATIONAL EXHIBITION. GLASGOW

Was it you
I saw last night
at the "Ex"?

Above: Hamilton's Aerial Railway, which can also be seen above the Whirlpool, passes between the Prince of Wales Bridge over the Kelvin and the church by the entrance to the Highland Village. The Aerial Railway was a novel idea giving an experience close to flying, but actually suspended on cables 130ft up in the air, moved by electricity, any avoiding anxiety about exploding gas for the passengers.

Left: 'Was it you I saw last night at the "Ex"'? Each exhibition spanning the Edward VII reign (which included the planning for the 1911 display) was a success, in popularity and profit. In 1901 Glasgow declared its Second City pride and during the decade the future seemed bright however 1911 marked an end to those peaceful years. Plenty of exhibitions may be memorable, but those lighthearted, confident days in Edwardian Kelvinside seemed unforgettable, as long as you survived what was soon to come.

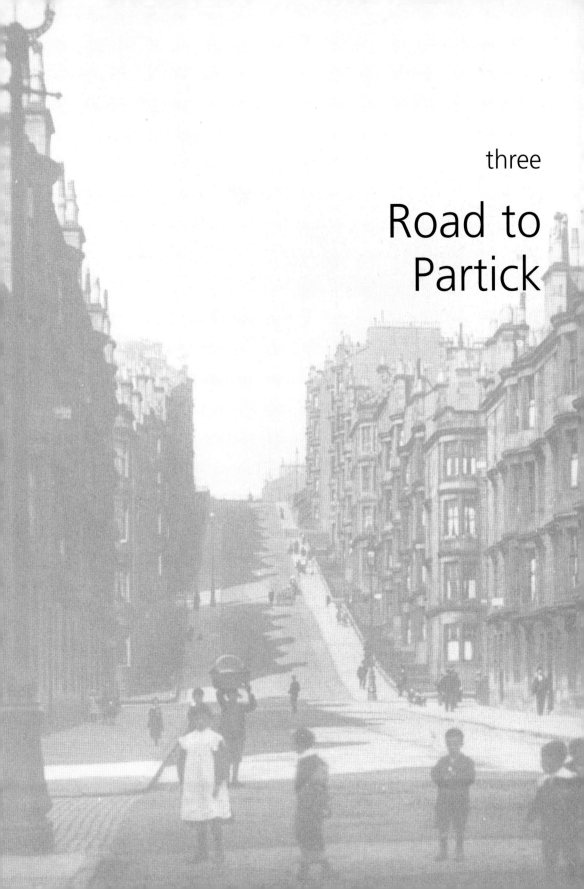

three

Road to
Partick

A view across Kelvingrove Park to the College Free Church on the left and the synagogue to the right of it. The former burnt down in 1925 and was never replaced. The latter lasted longer but closed some years after the war. Forty years or so later the remains of it slowly decay. The Kelvingrove Street entry to the park is before the church and beyond Argyll Street and the houses. Ships on the Clyde are just visible. (PPC: Taylor, Woodlands Road)

The Stewart Memorial Fountain in West End Park, 1904. The Corporation committee created West End Park and South Side Park in the nineteenth century, long known also as Kelvingrove and Queens Parks. The memorial has now been restored after many years. At the Exhibition of 1901 the Irish and Canadian Pavilions were situated here. (PPC: M. Wane)

Looking down from Park Terrace in 1905, John S. Kennedy's statue of a lion was the first of many statues and memorials to be seen in the park. He donated the lion and its young, an impressive sight, but their relationship to Mr Kennedy, a Scot living in New York, is not now clear. (PPC: Caledonia, 611).

University and Lord Roberts Monument, Glasgow.

Down the slope, trees hid most of the park in 1920 but not the monument to Lord Roberts VC, who, though already retired after a distinguished army career, died in France in 1914. The view beyond the park shows (extreme right), the Hillhead U.F. Church and just across University Avenue is a low line of shops, the future site of the university Men's Union. Wellington Church, higher up University Avenue, stands out. (PPC: Taylor's Woodlands Road)

THE BOWLING GREEN, KELVINGROVE PARK, GLASGOW.

WEST END ROLLER RINK
KELVINGROVE, GLASGOW.

The Fascinating Pastime.

Above: The Bowling Green in Kelvingrove Park in around 1925, near Kelvin Way and, in later days, next to the Museum and Art Gallery. Bowling was long established but often unfairly regarded by some as for serious old men. Park Terrace is seen in the distance with the Park Church and Trinity College standing out on the left. (PPC: Caledonia Series, 1268)

Left: An advertisement for the West End Roller Rink – 'The Fascinating Pastime'. It was one of the most popular indoor activities in the first decades of the last century and rinks appeared all over the country. This was something that was good exercise, good fun and gave a chance to mix with the other sex in something obviously innocent – at the time anyway. (PPC: Stafford & Co., Netherfield, Notts)

Opposite below: The Art Gallery in its earlier years might have been described as a bare display of humanity but in more recent years greater variety was shown here. At the start of the twenty-first century the building was closed for a complete renewal of the interior and a long-needed cleaning of the ceilings and the walls. The results were amazing when the century-old beauty was first displayed. (PPC: Reliable Series; J. Crawford)

Above: The Art Galleries and Kelvin Hall, looking east, 1930. Two prams on the left have just passed over the Kelvin to Dumbarton Road and a solitary tram makes its way into town. The Kelvin Hall, right, not long open, was built after its predecessor on this road went up in flames. This card was posted from the Theatre Royal by 'Nev' to his father, G.F. Painsley, in Oxford, who was seemingly an actor: 'Your letter was most interesting Dear Dad. Model arrived in London but broken, just my luck.' (PPC: Caledonia)

The original Kelvin Hall burnt down in around 1925. High winds carried sparks east from the burning building and set fire to the college and Kelvingrove Church (see p. 52) half a mile away. The much more successful replacement for the Kelvin Hall, which was soon built, attracted crowds to displays and entertainments of all sorts, all the year round, until the 1960s when many items were transferred elsewhere and part of the hall became the transport museum. The latter later moved into a new building along the river.

A Kelvin Hall Concert Party in 1920. Groups such as this would no doubt welcome the chance to display their talents in the towns and cities during the months when there was no work at the seaside. In 1920, cinemas, though improving every year, were still without sound, and radio had not yet reached the sitting room, though all these wonders would soon be available. (PPC: The Premier Studio, Paisley and Glasgow)

Kelvin Way, right to left from Argyle Street to University Avenue, crossing over the river, with Gray Street in the background, *c.* 1920. The bridge was hit by a bomb in 1941 and lost some of its corner sculptures but these were fortunately recovered and replaced. The bowlers are busy, but tennis has only one pair playing. (Caledonia)

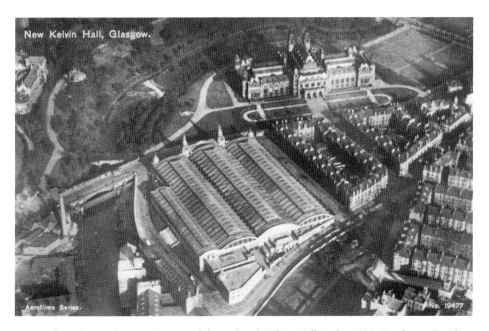

A view from the air showing the size of the replaced Kelvin Hall in the 1920s. Bunhouse Road by the Kelvin is on the left and Blantyre Street on the right. The Museum and Art Gallery has the river behind while the Old Dumbarton Road runs behind the new building and the original crossing of the river.

THE KELVIN HALL, GLASGOW.

The Kelvin Hall, seen here in the late 1930s, was showing a Housing and Health Exhibition as well as presenting the Kneller Hall Band. The red tram No. 327, a mere forty years on the road, is bound for Cambuslang, while Corporation bus No. 4 is on the No. 15 route to Knightswood. There is quite a crowd at the Kelvin Hall to see one of its attractions on what seems to be a chilly day. (PPC: Caledonia Series)

THE KELVIN HALL, FACADE, INDUSTRIAL POWER EXHIBITION, GLASGOW
FESTIVAL OF BRITAIN 1951

A TUCK CARD

The Festival of Britain in 1951, exactly one century after the famous London Exhibition, had as its main purpose to celebrate the recovery of Britain after the war and the six difficult years which had followed. The Industrial Power Exhibition was opened in the Kelvin Hall on 28 May by Princess Elizabeth, followed by a speech from a Westminster politician who declared that the display was a great credit to England.

The River Kelvin is crossed by Partick Bridge, previously the boundary with Glasgow. This photograph was taken on a calm day in 1924. The reflections in the water emphasise the beautiful design of the bridge, though it would be optimistic to expect the water quality at this time to be as attractive. There has been a crossing at this part of the river for more than 200 years but the ancient Old Dumbarton Road behind the Kelvin Hall still runs to Benalder Street by the weir. (PPC: Valentine X.L. Series, 92206)

Western Infirmary, Glasgow

The Western Infirmary in 1904. The main entrance on the Partick side of the river shows a spacious, open front which was eventually built on to provide facilities for medical research and development. Benefits to the public, before and after the NHS, continued until in the later years of the last century it was planned to replace the overcrowded and inconvenient site with one for modern departments. (PPC: Valentine)

Old Partick

This picture of 'Old Partick' shows Keith Street (earlier Kelvin Street) opposite Hyndland Street, across Dumbarton Road. The old weavers' houses were taken down in 1930. The building beyond the houses is John Forbes, Dyer and Cleaner. In the time of Partick village this street was called The Goat and this part was The Head of the Goat. (PPC: Valentine)

Bishop Mill Court, a nineteenth-century mill by the river, was built on the site of the first one erected in Partick and given to the Bishop of Glasgow. His mill replaced a much smaller one on the Molendilar. This newly named building has now been converted into flats. (W. Spalding)

St Peter's in Partick Bridge Street was the first Roman Catholic church in Partick, opened in 1858. Closed in 1903 when a church was built in Hyndland Street, it re-opened briefly twenty years later. The old church became a billiards and reading room but ten years later this was re-opened in the new St Simon's parish. Since the early days of the Second World War it has been used by the Polish community. On the left is the Chapel House and the old school is on the far right.

St Peter's RC School was built in 1899 and is seen here in 1905. The older boys were taught at the building in Hyndland Street, seen on the right. The front of the building along Dowanhill Street looks much the same today, a hundred years later, and it is still in use. The Gaelic church in Dowanhill Street can be seen on the left. (PPC: Valentine)

GARDNER STREET, PARTICK.

Gardner Street, rising north from Dumbarton Road, is one of the steepest in the city. This view from around 1913 shows the street's lower half with a variety of shops, including a laundry on the right, before the first crossing, while 'Dyers of Perth' are nearer to the camera. 'Cott's Bargains' can be had at the first shop on the left while further down the same side a once familiar red and white sign advertises a 'Hair Dressing Saloon'.

Gardner Street, Partick.

This later view, further from the main road, shows the new church on the left and Bulloch and Gardner, decorators and painters, on the right. The top of the street should be descended with care. In earlier days vehicles were tested for the safety of their brakes! (PPC: S.O. Anderson, Partick; Davidsons Quality, London)

This is Dumbarton Road with Peel Street on the left in 1929. A dentist and an artist are advertised on the corner and the man with a stick is passing R.S. McColl's, confectioners. Bus No. 117, for Riddrie, Route 11, is mentioned in the message on the reverse of this postcard, '... one of our new buses'. Also on the reverse, 'Our butcher is obviously Galloway', the hilarious subject of a memorable Glasgow play. By Galloway's is a newsagent selling Dobie's Roll Tobacco. On the other side is the corner with Merkland Street and 'Tyler's Popular Shop'.

Peel Street in 1909. The cricket ground halfway up, past St Mary's church, which is long gone as is the distant High Church, partly sold for housing. The first football international was played there (Scotland 0, England 0). The premises of 'Black, Plasterer', is on the left. The housing on the left was replaced but on the modified cricket ground playing the game continues. During the war Peel Street was hit by a land mine with some damage on the left. (PPC: Valentine, 54418)

Hamilton Crescent was renamed Fortrose Street in the 1920s, seen here in around 1912. The cricket ground boundary is on the left and Hamilton Crescent School is just visible through the trees. A young boy cycles down the middle of the otherwise empty road. (PPC: Caledonia 1183)

Hamilton Crescent School, Partick.

The school is now fully visible with a group of boys lined up for the photograph. It seems to have been taken before they were all in line or behaving themselves. The boy in front appears to be telling the others to come forward. On the left a boy with a kilt is between two smaller boys engrossed in some problem. This school is no more. (PPC: Davidson Bros, London)

Burgh Hall, Partick.

The Burgh Hall, in the street of the same name, before 1913. From the day that Partick's independence ceased, on 4 November 1912, its name has stood for many local activities and theatre. It was built in 1872 by the architect William Leiper, and is shown here before the Lesser Burgh Hall was added in 1913. Leiper also designed Dowanhill Church in Hyndland Street, now the Cottier Theatre. The church with the tall spire beyond the hall has long gone. (PPC: W.N. Coy's 'Record')

Partick Hill station in the early 1960s, when the station was by Crow Road, across Dumbartorn Road. It moved later in order that trains from the Central, Queen Street and the Subway could join opposite. The No. 9 tram, from Dalmuir West to Auchenshuggle, was the last to run before the buses took over in 1963. Trams were often blamed for slowing the traffic by stopping in the middle of the road for passengers. (A.J. Douglas)

BROOMHILL AVENUE, PARTICK WEST.

Broomhill Avenue is now cut short as the Clydeside Expressway merges into Victoria Park Drive South. For a mile Dumbarton Road is no longer the main road since the Clyde Tunnel opened. At the far end of the Avenue in this picture is Broomhill Drive at the crossroads from where West Broomhill Terrace East ran directly to Victoria Park. Opposite the top of this road now is a group of seventeen-storey buildings. (PPC: Miss I.G. Clarke, Partick West)

Broomhill Avenue, Partick West.

Broomhill Avenue again, from further back, showing the other side of the road. The near building is the swimming pool for Balshagray School, later to become an annex of Anniesland College. Both of these postcards date from Edwardian days and considerable changes have taken place, even before the tunnel was built nearby. A walk from here to nearby Victoria Park is somewhat noisier and less straightforward today than it was in the past.

Thornwood Drive, looking down to Dumbarton Road, *c.* 1910. The houses facing at the bottom of the road were taken down before the first huge Meadowside Granary was built. The second of these was erected as late as 1960, to be taken down not long after the end of the century. Thornwood Drive is one side of an early nineteenth-century development up a steep hill which drops down to the Crow Road/Clarence Drive junction. (PPC: I.G. Roxburgh)

Boys at the school between Thornwood Drive and Thornwood Avenue are seen playing football on a fine day in the 1970s. The old building can be seen to have been added to on the right side, in the style of the time. Below the football pitch there was a small pleasant open area for the local residents, now used for housing.

The Tivoli cinema in Crow Road, a short distance from Dumbarton Road, opened in 1929. The original 1900 auditorium seats were very spacious. It is remembered to have been dimly lit, in the intervals too, possibly connected with the row of double seats at the back, popular in early days for the 'spooners'. Taken over by the Gaumont in 1932 it was eventually sold to be a Classic but not before audiences were 'up' to *Rock Around the Clock* here in October 1959. (Kevin Wheelan)

Balshagray Farm, a scene from the past, by the junction of Crow Road with Balshagray Avenue, before the area was built up. The 'auld world hamlet of Balshagrie' by the mansion of Woodcroft was occupied until 1911. Victoria Park still provides the green grass and water there to enjoy. (PPC: Elsmores Series, No.2)

four

Anniesland
and
Jordanhill

Above: Kirklee Road, past the Botanic Gardens, 1938. A broad road with large houses which can only be described as 'greatly desirable', often divided up into smaller residences in their second century. The blue tram (No. 483), dating from 1903, ran from the terminus to Rutherglen. In the 1940s the route was extended to Hyndland Road and the Kirklee rails were removed. The car, registration No. G125, is emerging from Kirklee Terrace. (W.A. Camwell)

Left: The female conductress was first seen in the First World War as male Glasgow tramcar staff volunteered to fight in great numbers at the outbreak of war. In most cities the 'lady conductors' (the men were never known as 'gentlemen') were sent home with thanks when men returned, but some in Glasgow remained. (Photograph by Weir)

Right: Sir Henry Campbell-Bannerman, Prime Minister from 1905 to 4 April 1908, one week before he died. His father, Sir James Campbell, was Glasgow Lord Provost 1840-43 and Sir Henry, after adding 'Bannerman' to his name, became the Stirling Liberal MP from 1868. Kelvinside House, his birthplace, was in the Botanic Gardens by the far side of Kelvin River. This postcard is postmarked 1907.

SIR HENRY CAMPBELL-BANNERMAN.
Prime Minister of Great Britain.

Below: Kelvinside Academy, private school at Bellshaugh Road, off Kirklee Road, opened in 1878 and looks hardly different now from this 1904 view. Pupils from here often went into business but from the 1920s more entered university, going on to Oxford or Cambridge to study for law. The school has been co-educational since 1998. The message on the reverse of the postcard is complimentary: 'Having a good time here. I had a nice walk by the side of the Kelvin this afternoon. Weather could not be better.' (PPC: Caledonia Series, 412)

Old KELVINSIDE HOUSE, GLASGOW. Birthplace of Sir Henry Campbell Bannerman.

Highburgh Road, from Byres Road and, nowadays, opposite University Avenue, rises to Hyndland Road to enter that Edwardian suburb. On the right side is a small park, the 'Wee Park', which dates from 1903 when the Burgh of Partick reserved the site that would otherwise have been taking for housing.

Minard Road, known as Turnberry Road since the 1920s when the city revised many street names to get rid of duplication. The road runs straight for a quarter of a mile to end where the railway from Partick crosses. The tramline is on the curve of Hyndland Road as it flattens out on its way to Great Western Road

Hyndland Road with the top of Clarence Drive on the left where the distant tram is seen. This housing and line of shops from the 1910s is still easily recognisable today. The electric trams were by then well established but only horse traffic is otherwise in sight. The tram terminus was later moved further along, nearer Great Western Road.

Clarence Drive crosses under the railway after descending from Broomhill Cross. The Hyndland Secondary School in the Airlie Building (top left) dates from 1912 when the Hyndland houses were established. The bus, No 18 (GD7575), was one of the earliest in the Corporation fleet in the later 1920s. Destined for St Vincent Street, it has stopped for a man while across the road a young boy is cycling up on the wrong side.

CROW ROAD. BROOMHILL CROSS

Broomhill Cross, c. 1910. This is where Clarence Drive (then Blenheim Drive) and Churchill Drive enter Crow Road, which runs south to Dumbarton Road, north to Anniesland. A. Cochrane, tea dealer, at the corner is selling tea for 1s 4d to 2s 2d a quarter and advertises Bovril, among many other things. A baker, a chemist and a tobacconist occupy the other shops – what more could be needed? An old-fashioned police box is on the corner. (PPC: J. Duncan, 252 Crow Road)

CROW ROAD, GLASGOW

The row of houses seen above was eventually extended along the road as seen here in 1960. Marlborough Avenue, crossing Crow Road, leads down towards Balshagray Avenue, but no longer reaches it today to pass over to Victoria Park since through traffic now goes on its way south to the Clyde Tunnel (see p. 92). Beyond the houses on the left the tennis ground was established in the 1920s. (PPC: Valentine D5076)

Hyndland Road, Glasgow.

Hyndland Road with Clarence Drive in the distance and Novar Drive going off to the right beyond the shops. Built in the early twentieth century, the red sandstone flats, a compact area, were slow to sell at first, but soon became desirable homes. The shops are, from the left: Dunn; J. Chalvers & Co.; Buttercup for Butter & Tea: T. Macmaster; James Boag; Brown, for clothing, and F.H. Chisholm, who sold this postcard from his shop. The railway terminus, now gone, was to the right of the shops. (PPC: Woodlands Series)

Westbourne Gardens, Kelvinside

F. W. FYFE, PARTICKHILL

Westbourne Gardens, parallel and close to Hyndland Road from Great Western Road, is seen here in 1908. The scene a hundred years later is hardly changed although in this century the Free Church is Struthers Memorial Pentecost. The building on its right, later hidden even more by trees, also survives. (PPC: F.W. Fyfe, Partickhill)

Polwarth Gardens (Street) runs parallel to Hyndland Road and is seen here in 1911. The Hyndland Bowling Club is on the right and Novar Drive in the distance. In 2005 the club celebrated its centenary. The trees seen in front of the building have continued to grow so the clubhouse is now well protected. Polwarth Street otherwise looks much as it was, if today's cars are ignored. (PPC: Valentine 69778)

Dudley Drive, across Clarence Drive, just above the railway crossing, was one of the first tenement buildings constructed in the area in 1898, the first few closes being in Partick Burgh. The tenements are less ornate than the later ones. Garden railings seen behind the children here in 1905 were of a Victorian style not repeated. The grass in the middle of the road has been removed in this section, but remains across Clarence Drive. In 1941 five houses in the street were demolished by bombs. (PPC: Hartmann)

The Cavendish Hotel, 1 Devonshire Gardens at the Hyndland Road corner, is shown here in 1953 and described by the sender of the postcard as 'very Victorian, but nice'. Some time later it became, and has remained for many years, *the* hotel for the well known and the well off, and keeps its fame and dignity while extending down the road. It remains 'very nice'.

Great Western Road, with Hyndland Road behind the tram on the left, and Cleveland Road on the right, 1907. Beyond this point the road was less developed on the north side; the Royal Mental Hospital (later Gartnavel General) and its ground had taken much of the south side further down. Bingham's Pond, used for skating and curling or rowing, is now halved in size for a restaurant and garage. Further on rugby is played. The tram, No. 904, was scrapped in 1958. (PPC: Valentine, 57467)

Glasgow Homeopathic Hospital, just past Cleveden Road, was for many years in this impressive building at No. 1000, the only such hospital in Glasgow or elsewhere. Independence in medicine in recent years has become difficult to manage. This 1934 postcard bears a mysterious message: 'I have been looking every day for word about the blankets ... what is wrong ... let me know. All have the cold.' Lets hope they arrived. (PPC: Weir)

Whittingehame Gardens lies along the road, beyond the boating pond, while Whittingehame Drive branches off on the left, to meet Crow Road. This picture dates from the 1910s and the space behind the grand houses was developed in following years. The road here had became two-way by the 1930s with trams in the centre. (PPC: Anniesland Post Office)

Above: Houses in Kelvindale Road, 1950s. The builder of these, the first houses (Nos 343-5) in the road in the late 1920s was soon bankrupt. The road, an ancient lane to Maryhill on the Kelvindale private estate, was off Rossloan (later Cleveden) Road, which ran north from Great Western Road to the canal. A revised and more ambitious housing development on this large site was soon built in Kelvindale with English town and city road names and art deco decoration, now mostly gone. The result was a successful private achievement, which was added to after the war.

Right: Road building south of Kelvindale. This photograph is dated 1937, but apart from the high lamp posts, it could have been taken in the earliest days of photography. Shovels, picks and patient horses seem oddly out of place here, at a time in the city when elsewhere the great art deco Empire Exhibition was to be presented in the following year. (JGS)

Cleveden Road, which runs from Great Western Road across Kelvindale and over the canal. Passing the shops in the centre of this housing district is a well-filled horse-drawn cart. The nearest shop is an outfitter. The houses in the Kelvindale of the 1920s and '30s often incorporated art deco designs. (PPC: Caledonia)

Southampton Drive, half of an inner crescent, showing the current style on the doors and windows of the houses. Each crescent had its own designs. The road surface here appears not to have been finished. The mixed names of English roads and avenues include a wide variety such as the little Devon village Ashburton and cities such as Manchester and Northampton. (PPC: Caledonia)

Highfield Avenue, on the opposite side of Cleveden Road, is seen here curling round at the far end into the circular Baronald Drive. Identical designs appear all down the street but differ from the previous examples in Southampton Drive. By the twenty-first century much of the art deco design on these houses had disappeared. (PPC: Caledonia Series)

Highfield Avenue and a more detailed look at Nos 114 and 118. The building presumably holds four houses, with two other doors at the sides. This postcard picture is something of a mystery, published by G. Gilfillan, Lawrence Street, designed similar to that of Highfield Drive. The only postcard photographs published on Kelvindale in the 'Caledonia Series' were produced in about 1930 but those posted were mostly sold around 1960.

Baronald Drive, a circular road with Lindsay Road dividing it, has houses with the same outside features as Highfield Avenue. At the end of the short Endfield Avenue a little boy and girl are out for a walk with dog and tricycle, and a man walks down the opposite side of the road. The roads shown in all these early Kelvindale photographs show little life.

Winchester Drive (although this postcard says 'Road') runs parallel to Cleveden Road from Southampton Drive to Ashburton Road. The art deco designs are again different. This 1931 card to Ron from Ray in Whitley Bay tells of his stay in Glasgow: 'Having a great time, the weather being OK up till now I have just got 4 golf balls already. Saw *Hell's Angels* last night and have just got back from seeing the Rangers play.' *Hells Angels,* made in 1930 by Howard Hughes, was one of the first big film 'talkie' spectaculars and much talked about at the time.

ESQUIRE HOUSE, GREAT WESTERN ROAD, ANNIESLAND, GLASGOW

This is Esquire House on Great Western Road, between First Avenue and the railway bridge, built in the late 1950s and seen here in 1963. It was a popular place for meetings or guests for many years but by this century it had been replaced by a taller public house of a bland brick design. (PPC: Valentine D8148)

Great Western Road, Anniesland

The North British, but now long since Anniesland, station, 1905. British Rail(ways) took over in 1947 from LMS. Advertisements under the bridge suggest what to buy; some of these are still with us but Waldemar Pianos, Woodward Ho! for a smoke and Globe Polish have all gone. A1 Sauce is only known in the USA and whatever it was that Kills Fleas, Moths, Bugs, Beetles, is surely still needed! The road stopped here until the 1920s. (PPC: Anniesland Post Office)

The Ascot, Anniesland, a great art deco cinema built in1939 and the end of an era. Wonderful in all ways, it had 1,900 wide seats, lush carpets, air conditioning, magic lighting and in some ways a final memory of the previous year's Empire Exhibition. A Gaumont later, later still an Odeon, by the 1990s it had sunk into being a Bingo. The twenty-first century sees its front as of old, with equally luxurious homes built behind, where the ghostly grown-ups and Saturday's matinee children once paid to see the magic.

Great Western Road looking west from the station, c. 1920. The building across the road has not yet been extended - the gap was not filled for decades. Crow Road crossed the main road and ran for half-a-mile past printing works and iron works and to housing on the left side. For a long time that part of Crow Road was cut off from the roundabout. (PPC: H. McElroy)

The top of Crow Road in early Edwardian days with distant Belvedere Plantations over the railway and canal. Temple Place now has modern houses and Dawsholm Park is beyond the canal. A rail track ran by the canal and past the timber yard before curling round to Anniesland Road and Knightswood Hospital. Left of the horse and cart, 'Provisions' and 'Cadbury's Cocoa' are advertised. The X above the houses marks the flat of the sender, 'below is our happy little home'. (PPC: Anniesland P.O.)

Temple Gardens, seen here in 1918, were very high-quality Edwardian flats built in a busy manufacturing area and a century later looking as new. Housing a further half-mile to the left on Fulton Street was later extended and now crosses Bearsden Road and continues to Knightswood Cross. (PPC: Andrew Wardrop, Temple P.O.)

Barr & Stroud, the famous business in the Temple area which moved across the Clyde after the Second World War. The seventeen men shown here in 1915 worked in the Experimental Department during the First World War. The company described its business at the time as in 'Fortress, Naval and Field Rangefinders, Electric Clocks, High Vacuum Pumps and Electric Ship Telegraphs'.

All Saints Church on Crow Road above Anniesland Cross, seen before the First World War. The Methodist church was dismantled and rebuilt in 1928 on the left side of the newly built Bearsden Road but without the top line of windows. Also in this area 'Collars' cleaned for shirts all over Britain till the 1960s when separate collars became no longer the thing as the air cleaned and the 'Collars' collapsed.

Anniesland Mansion in Great Western Road curves into Crow Road. The tram terminus has No. 289 waiting to set off to the city. This particular tram, built in 1909, served till 1960 and has been in the Tramway Museum ever since. The building is new, with shops at the corner 'To Let' and a 'Factor's Office' round the corner, beside the dentist. (PPC: H. McElroy)

Anniesland Cross, 1936. Little changed looking towards town, or for many years, but big changes have taken place westward to Knightswood. The Welsh red, white and yellow metal pavement Keep Left warnings were later replaced by plastic, probably less dangerous when hit. On Crow Road, above the tram terminus, is a Grain Store. (PPC: Valentine A4140)

ANNIESLAND CROSS FROM GROW ROAD, GLASGOW.

Bearsden Road, which did not exist before the late twenties, is seen over the Cross to the left of the tent. Great Western Road had extended west serving the newly built Knightswood houses and continuing much further. New houses can also be seen in the distance with the modern Cyro factory, nearer, served by the railways, with wagons waiting. This picture from the late 1920s shows much energetic work in the area. (PPC: Valentine A4141)

Anniesland Cross in 1960. The trams had recently been replaced by buses but not much else in the scene had changed for years. There was still a gap in the housing on the north side and the traffic is still fairly light. The removal of the tramline across the roundabout, regarded then as a nuisance, was followed by alterations to the crossing shortly after the buses took over. (PPC: Valentine D5078)

Woodend Drive in Jordanhill, a short distance down Crow Road, in around 1908. Looking from Bordon Road (No. 38), the houses above have changed little as has the Jordanhill Parish Church or the Episcopal All Saints Church in the distance. The sender of the postcard to a friend in Plymouth explains that his house is 'opposite to the nearer church, with the tower'.

Jordanhill College and School entrance on Chamberlain Road, opposite Woodend Drive, 1920s. The College Training Centre is in the distance. Since the time of the photograph much has developed and the college is now part of Glasgow University. It has continued to expand and is now completely separate from the school, which still runs very successfully. (Woodlands Series)

Jordanhill station where the North British Railway crossed Crow Road, going west from Glasgow, c. 1905. The station is now unmanned, with the platforms somewhat reduced in length and all buildings gone. Children are on the bridge waiting for a train but all else is quiet here.

Beechwood Drive, opposite Abbey Drive in Jordanhill where Balshagray Road goes off Crow Road, c. 1905. The houses, a century later, look little changed today except that the end of the road is blocked off from the busy junction. House No. 1 started here at the main road, but the numbering has been turned around with the end houses now in the 150s. No. 1 was a surgery with Dr W.A. Caskie's name displayed on the lamppost and twice on the corner of the road. (PPC: W. Ross)

Abbey Drive, Jordanhill.

Above: Abbey Drive, off Crow Road at Balshagray Avenue, originally curved into Brunswick Avenue, which no longer exists, going south to Victoria Park. It now runs only to the school between it and Westland Drive. The whole plan of this area has been altered since the taking of this photograph in 1924. (PPC: J.H. Mackie, Jordanhill)

Right: Manor Road lies between Orlean Avenue and Eastcote Avenue but 100 years ago they were known as Kent and York Avenues, before Partick joined Glasgow. 'Jack', from No. 1, wrote a long letter on the reverse of this card to Mrs Vinis in Peckham, advising that 'Rob, smart little chap will grow more robust and strong – give him plenty of fresh air. Same as we are getting for it, it is blowing hard and a most respectable man coming home from church has just had his hair blown off'!

Victoria Park Gardens North in 1948. There were few cars around in the post-war years and even now this road is much more peaceful than the South Drive, below the park, since Dumbarton Road traffic was switched there. All over Britain, from 1940, garden railings were taken away, the metal supposedly to be for making Spitfires, and so bushes replaced them. (PPC: Valentine B627)

Victoria Park Gardens South Road remains open to Balshagray Avenue today. Many streets on the very busy main road are now blocked but this crossroad survives. This 1916 view was posted in 1948 from 'Ardragowan', the house shown at No. 76 Balshagray Avenue: 'I thought you might like to see Auntie Ina's home'. Just in time perhaps; the 1907 Congregational church is closed and this magnificent home has gone. It was destroyed to widen the road many years ago and only grass and trees now occupy the site. (PPC: Valentine 81378)

Balshagray Avenue, Whiteinch.

Above: Balshagray Avenue, off Dumbarton Road, opposite the short Inchholm Street, leading to Milton Street and Saw Mill Road, *c.* 1908. All have gone since the Clyde Tunnel was built. It now passes straight down from the junction at Victoria Park Drive South. This view of a quiet road bears only a horse-drawn 'Castlebank' van, collecting and delivering clothes for cleaning. The Aitken & Reid shop sold sheets and bedding. Beyond the van and the church is the Victoria Park. (PPC: 'Record', W.N. Coy)

VICTORIA PARK, GLASGOW

Above: Victoria Park (or Whiteinch Park) with two little girls looking across the small pond towards the war memorial in 1948. A few hopeful waterfowl are up to the edge looking for food to be thrown to them. There are two small islands in the pond for the birds and there was a larger artificial loch for model yacht sailing. (PPC: Valentine, B630)

Right: The war memorial, erected after the First World War to: 'Our Beloved Dead – Remembrance of the Men of Partick and Whiteinch who fell in the Great War 1914 – 1918'. This postcard is dated 1927. The names of those remembered following the Second World War were added on the back of the memorial.

Opposite below: Park Drive South, looking west, and peaceful in 1924. It is winter and it may have been snowing. Since the 1960s this has been the main road, with a mile of Dumbarton Road now blocked off at the east end. (PPC: Reliable Series, 1924)

War Memorial, Whiteinch Park

New (or Fossil) Grove was the unexpected consequence of planning a road through the bottom of a quarry in 1887. This Edwardian picture illustrates the quarry which was found to contain many fossilized tree stumps and was made into a popular park area. The man sitting down is in uniform and may be a park worker. (PPC: Caledonia)

Grove House, as it was called, shown here before the glass roof was added, 1911. The rest of the building is seemingly covered and almost hidden by the trees. The contents, the fossils, represent only a minute bit of an ancient tropical forest from the Carboniferous Period. There are eleven stumps of various sizes, the tallest showing 90cm above the rock floor. (PPC: Valentine 69260)

The fossil tree stumps, about 300 million years old, are of trees not found in modern times. The building dates from 1890. Above the tree stumps a Cist cemetery from the Middle Bronze Age was found during the work to expose the finds. This picture dates back about 100 years and the building has been much improved since then, outside and in.

The quarry in the 1960s, now a beautiful, quiet garden in the southwest corner of the park. It's a peaceful place to be in the summer, unless children are playing hide and seek on the narrow paths between the great high stones! The building covering the tree stumps is seen above the steps, the present entry being at the far end.

Paddle Boats, Whiteinch Park.

Close to the model yacht pond was a place for paddle boats, a popular enjoyment for all ages, especially the youngsters, in the park. The boats seen here in 1925 are being well used. They were not supposed to sail beyond the bridge.

Bandstand, Whiteinch Park.

The bandstand in Whiteinch Park was built in 1908 and a brick bow was added later. Music in town parks now seems to be wanted less and the bandstand in this park is no more.

Camperdown Road, now Earlbank Avenue (*c.* 1917) runs parallel to Dumbarton Road between Lennox Avenue and Victoria Drive, part of an early twentieth-century housing area in Scotstoun, which at the time was on the boundary with Yoker. The ancient Clyde ferry to Renfrew remains in use for pedestrians. In the past, Yoker was situated on both sides of the Clyde. (PPC: Caledonia)

Duncan Avenue, seen across Dumbarton Road in early Edwardian times. The local school on Camperdown Road (now Earlbank Avenue) has the Scotstoun Showground behind, known originally as the Glasgow Agricultural Society Show Ground, on Danes Avenue. The tram is making from Dalmarnock to Partick.

Stuart Avenue, Scotstoun

4059/37

Stuart (now Verona) Avenue was the most westerly in the area. The continuing growth of trees has improved many of these attractive streets off Dumbarton Road. The once busy works on the riverside of the road is now quiet. West of Whiteinch is no longer in Partick but into Yoker.

WHITEINCH CAR TERMINUS.

Whiteinch tramcar terminus, 1911. Trams turned on the left at Primrose Street, opposite the Bowling Club and, behind the horse and coal cart, are Whiteinch station and mineral depot. The man on the right is a tram inspector and he has a young lad assistant opposite. Boys wearing Eton collars help with something to be hauled across the road, watched by a young boy with bare feet, something often seen in Glasgow, right into the 1920s. A woman wearing the ubiquitous shawl of the period is beyond them. (PPC: R. Macleod, Crow Road)

Victoria Drive curving south from Anniesland Road to Dumbarton Road in 1913. Only a few houses were built on the left side before the rail crossing under the road, at the top. As the Knightswood development extended, Victoria Drive crossed to connect with Lincoln Avenue, north to Great Western Road a mile or so beyond Anniesland. (PPC: Valentine 76813 – 1913, J.M. Gray, Stationer)

Anniesland Road, 1912. This road skirted the land of Scotstoun House to the east on its way to Dumbarton Road but by the 1930s Kingsway provided a direct route after Scotstounhill station and the old route became quieter. The road down from Anniesland has a range of housing of various designs. (PPC: Valentine 72499)

DUMBARTON ROAD, SCOTSTOUN, WEST.

Above: Yoker Road (later Dumbarton Road) looking west to Anniesland Road, 1911. This was then beyond the Partick boundary and was not yet lined with houses. On the left is the entrance to a private house. This section of road was soon to be lined with houses on the north side and on the space between it and the rails on the other side. (PPC: Caledonia – R. Macleod, Crow Road)

Right: A rainy summer day on Dumbarton Road in 1960. The No. 9 tram making its way across the city to Auchenshuggle is on the long route from Dalmuir West. In three years time the last of them will sway away off the streets forever. The Corporation bus behind might last a little longer, until private companies would took over the job. The church on the right has been replaced by houses.

Opposite below: Merklands Quay, next to Meadowside Quay, seen from the air with the Merklands Lairage, where cattle were housed, beside Sawmill Road by the river. The Meadowside Granary is on the extreme right and the rails ran along Castlebank Street and South Street after crossing Dumbarton Road on the way south. Those lines were closed for passengers in the 1960s in favour of the route further inland while rail at the quayside was already being taken over by road vehicles.

Above: Partick West station, by Meadowside Quay, 1958. About 300 yards from Partick Cross, trucks to the Lanarkshire coalfields delivered the coal to Dumbarton, via Glasgow. The closing of shipyards saw the end of this rail and the passenger station closed. The Meadowside Granary is on the left, beyond the rails. Earlier in the century John Thomlinson Ltd, printers and carton makers, occupied that site. The two granaries erected between 1911 and 1962 closed in 1988 and are now gone.

Dumbarton Road, looking east in about 1957. The church on the left was on the far side of Victoria Drive. Among the line of shops was one of the popular Galbraith Stores, with Galloway's beside it. Beyond a Capstan advertisement on the next building is the big Domestos truck with a cafe by it. The post office is further along. These shops remain today though perhaps a little more colourful looking nowadays. (Valentine D2452)

A steam train crosses Yoker Road pulling a line of trucks to the docks, c. 1922. Burnham Terrace is seen from a different aspect with the Parish Council Chambers opposite at the end of Lasmuir Drive. The chambers were here in the days when Yoker looked after itself; the building looks as good as ever today and probably cleaner. It is now Plean Street Clinic. (PPC: S. Whitty, Burnham Terrace P.O.)

Dumbarton Road approaches the rail crossing with Burnham Road on this side. Burnham Terrace with its considerable line of shops seems busy with three horse-drawn deliveries attending. The one on the right is delivering coal, a sight common all over the city well into the sixties. Crossing the road on the left is a man on his way to clean the chimneys. (PPC: Caledonia; R. Henderson, 595 Yoker Road)

A closer view of Burnham Terrace and the other side of the building. On the front is the Yoker Road sign above the tea-room in front of which men and boys are lined up, perhaps just to be in the picture. To its right is a stationer, advertising 'Black & White' on the door. Burnham Road is down the left side of the building to South Street, after passing the station and under the rails. That railway route, though, is no longer. (PPC: Caledonia)

Above and below: Blawarthill Terrace, on the street of that name, *c.* 1910. This is another small connection to Langholm Street near the Renfrew Ferry. This tea-room, with dinners available, was also a newspaper shop. The illustration below shows the Terrace above Langholm Street and crossing rail track on the way to Rothesay Dock. Yoker is on the edge of Clydebank and housing around suffered from the 1941 bombing. Some of these attractive homes in this community off the main road suffered and not all survived. (PPC: A. McCorkindale, Blawarthill Terrace)

YOKER FERRY

Yoker Ferry, an ancient, day and night, crossing over the Clyde to Renfrew until the tunnel under the water to Govan, and the bridge over it from Old Kilpatrick, were built. It remains in action, but not for cars or trucks. In 1947, when this photograph was taken, there were few new cars to buy, unless you were a general practitioner or a politician. The two cars, the older FG8360 and the Ford XS3746 from across the water at Renfrew, are first out, with the two vans to follow, GD3405, a Glasgow number on an old Glasgow van and the more modern AZ52339, an Irish visitor. (PPC: Holmes)

Partick Pier (right) with the Govan Ferry No.3 (left) crossing the river, *c.* 1904. The pier was at the entry of the River Kelvin at the Partick border with Glasgow. It was built for paddlers after the Lochgoil disaster. The ferry closed in 1966. (PPC: Reliable)

Elderslie Hall by the river is seen here with a First World War memorial, on the Renfrew side, in the 1920s. Yoker's history was on both sides of the Clyde, next to Clydebank on the north side. The war memorial has now been moved to the Recreational Ground by Dumbarton Road near to the ferry.

Dumbarton Road, approaching the border with Clydebank after which its name changes to Glasgow Road. This almost empty road is seen here on a summer's day in 1955 with the remains of a petrol station on the left, an earlier victim of the Blitz. A tram is coming round the corner in the distance. In many ways the view looks much the same today but the petrol station has been reopened and is a large and busy one.

six

Knightswood
and
Drumchapel

Knightswood Hospital.

ATHELSTANE ROAD, KNIGHTSWOOD, GLASGOW.

The Boulevard as Vogue in the 1950s. (Strathclyde Regional Archives)

The Boulevard (later the Vogue) Cinema in Great Western Road, not far from Anniesland, was opened by William Beresford Inglis in 1928. Built in a Spanish-American style, with white stucco, hacienda windows above the entrance and an interior, described as 'a glorious Hollywood Andalusian courtyard'. It was a Western-style spectacle with stained-glass windows, ornamental balconies, lanterns, a pantile roof and a powder blue ceiling sky. Inglis sold his cinema to build the famous high, yellow and red Beresford Hotel in Sauchiehall Street, a war time favourite with visiting GIs and their girlfriends. After some alterations and more seating the Singletons reopened the cinema in 1939. It closed twenty years later, the site being taken over by B&Q. (Courtesy Mitchell Library City Archive, Glasgow City Council and thanks to Bruce Peter for the history.)

Opposite above: Knightswood Infectious Hospital, Anniesland Road, *c.* 1904. This hospital had a history from the nineteenth century and was very busy at a time when common infections or minor injuries often become serious or fatal illnesses. The introduction of seemingly magic treatments in the '30s and '40s, from routine preventive injections for children, penicillin for so many infections and the first real control for tuberculosis in 1951, emptied and eventually closed hospitals such as Knightswood. (PPC: J. Marshall, Scotstoun)

Opposite below: Athelstane Road is just below Knightswood Cross and Great Western Road. Since the early days, this road has been lined with trees, now long matured. Knightswood Road was originally the name of an ancient way north-west to Cloberhill Bridge on the canal, towards Drumchapel. Knightswood was the name given to the housing development between the wars and after the 1950s. 'Knightswood' settled into being just a part of the city, with its own attractions.

KNIGHTSWOOD COMMUNITY CENTRE

Knightswood Community Centre, off Alderman Road, was planned before the war and building had already started in 1939 but it was not completed until the 1950s. The building is very much to a pre-war design contrasting with the later, bleaker look of much of the sixties and seventies, though post-war additions to the building have been in keeping. (PPC. R. Tuck & Sons)

GOLF COURSE, KNIGHTSWOOD

The Knightswood Golf Course, seen here on a summer's day in the 1950s. The good planning and completion of the Knightswood housing estates surrounding the park was well established until war interrupted progress but it continued according to plan when materials became available again. Bowls and other sports were played and enjoyed in the great Knightswood Park. (PPC: R. Tuck & Sons)

DUNWAN AVENUE, KNIGHTSWOOD

Dunwan Avenue is a short street between Kelso Street and Dyke Road. These early wide main roads bordering most of the Avenues, Drives and minor roads have proved to be very successful. The new Knightswood community of modern, Corporation houses with gardens was in great contrast to the crowded, often decaying, nineteenth-century city slums. The No. 11 bus and a cyclist approach the junction with Kelso Street. (PPC: R. Tuck & Sons)

ST. BRENDAN'S CHURCH, KELSO STREET, KNIGHTSWOOD

St Brendan's Roman Catholic Church in Kelso Street which descends from the canal to Dumbarton Road, opposite the Yoker Ferry. The church is opposite Dunwan Avenue and the school. The flat-topped houses beyond the church are of post-war design. In the new century St Brendan's continues to be as busy and confident as when it first opened. (PPC: R. Tuck & Sons)

KILLOCH DRIVE, KNIGHTSWOOD

Killoch Drive, going south-west from Dyke Road, a street of houses typical of the 1930s period with four units to a block. Caldwell Avenue is on the right. A very small child is standing in the middle of the road beyond the parked car on the left – a fairly safe thing to do, perhaps, in the first years after the war. (PPC: R. Tuck & Sons)

Houses in Glanderston Drive can be seen in the background of this view, seen from the end of Commore Drive. Clarion Road turns off to the right. This is an early picture of the housing developments here that later continued across the open field in the centre of the view. The Garscadden Burn passes under Glanderston Drive along the edge of the golf course which is in the lower part of Knightswood Park.

DYKE ROAD SHOPS, KNIGHTSWOOD

Shops on Dyke Road, Knightswood, between Killoch Street and Alderman Road in the 1950s. A Fullotone van (FUS367) is outside Lanham, the greengrocer, and two ladies, one with a pram, have met outside the post office. Meat from Brechin Brothers and provisions from 'Tom' are available next door. The narrow shop front next to them is the Clydebank Co-op Society Ltd. On the corner with Killoch Street a lady glances into the tobacconist's window. (PPC: R. Tuck & Sons)

DYKE ROAD, KNIGHTSWOOD

Dyke Road, looking north, above the Blawarthill Hospital towards Alderman Road. In the distance the Campsie Hills can clearly be seen. Most main roads around here today, like this one, are busier, but the houses, now often privately owned, seem little altered outside, showing how well built they were. (PPC: R. Tuck & Sons)

Killoch Drive, looking down from Dyke Road, with Polnoon Avenue crossing it at the junction. This view is from the 1930s with the garden railings still intact. The compulsory loss of iron railings from gardens all over Britain was said to be used to make Spitfires to bring down the enemy.

Bankhead School is off Killoch Street on Caldwell Avenue. The house in the middle distance has now gone and was replaced by the school main entrance, joining together the two separate departments seen here.

Right: St David's Parish Church on Boreland Drive, near Lincoln Avenue, in a photograph from the 1950s. It still looks as new today. It is of the modern design of the time, when post-war optimism was high for Knightswood and the rest of the world. Churches today seem rarely to be built reaching high in the sky. (PPC: R. Tuck & Sons)

Below: Loanfoot Avenue lies along the lower edge of the golf course from Dyke Road and is parallel to Boreland Drive. The building on the near left lies just below St David's and belongs to the church but has not recently been in use. Until the 1950s, though, this building had itself been St David's Church, from 1929, when Knightswood and the park were laid down. Before this there had been a railway line crossing the area taking coal from a small local mine.

Loanfoot Avenue, Knightswood, Glasgow.

Polnoon Avenue, off Alderman Road, near Garscadden station, seen here in pre-war days. In earlier years residents had little opportunity to individualise houses and gardens on these estates. The city owned the houses and one could not interfere very much with their designs so uniformity ruled.

OVERLOOKING KNIGHTSWOOD PARK

Overlooking Knightswood Park to the north with the Campsies in the distance. Archerhill Road from left to right across the view divides the golf course from the public. In the distance is Great Western Road and in the park the miniature golf course can just be seen in the distance and tennis courts and bowling greens are nearer. (PPC: R. Tuck & Sons)

KNIGHTSWOOD PARK

Knightswood Park in the 1950s with two young boys looking down at the stream which runs up the side of that part of the park, facing onto Basset Avenue. The stream crosses under Archerhill Road to turn west toward Dyke Road. The park has been a great benefit to Knightswood, especially since temptation to build here has been resisted. (PPC: R. Tuck & Sons)

TENNIS COURTS AND SPORTS PAVILION, KNIGHTSWOOD PARK

Tennis Courts and the Sports Pavilion, Knightswood Park, looking north with Basset Avenue on the left and Chaplet Avenue behind the Pavilion. The sports facilities in the park were well used. Twenty or so years after the peace of 1945 times were still hard for many, but these idyllic scenes of the park record a time when life seemed to be settled and happy. (PPC: R. Tuck & Sons)

CHILDREN'S PLAYGROUND. KNIGHTSWOOD PARK

The childrens' playground in the park. The dozen or two young ones seem to be enjoying themselves, except for the girl sitting by herself on the roundabout with a toddler lying down. Some rather older ones are swinging high and the younger ones down below look happy. Perhaps nowadays it might all be thought to be too dangerous an enjoyment. (PPC: R. Tuck & Sons)

The Forth & Clyde Canal over Great Western Road, through Knightswood, *c.* 1951. House construction had started behind the pre-war Old Drumchapel by the main road and the canal. The canal bridge had foiled a plan in the 1920s to extend the tram route from Anniesland, for four miles, to meet the Clydebank route along Kilbowie Road to Duntocher.

Drumchapel post office on Garscadden Road, just past the railway. Before the twentieth century Drumchapel was a few houses by the North British Railway station from Glasgow. This building has survived to the present century, with a modern addition. The Great Western Road did not exist past Anniesland until the 1920s after which modern housing appeared from the road to Garcadden Road on the way from Bearsden to Clydebank. (PPC: Goldie's Series)

Royal Hospital for Sick Chldren, Country Branch, on Drumchapel Road, a quarter of a mile from Bearsden, in Edwardian days. The ageing hospital was converted after the war to private use for the elderly but by the start of the present century was demolished and a larger, modern residential home was built, with a further, independent home on the same site. Perhaps some of the sick children from the 1920s may have returned to stay here again.

Left: The war memorial and parish church, Drumchapel, 1934. As new housing developed in the area after the Second World War, the church eventually became redundant and the war memorial was moved to be next to the new church by the corner of Drumchapel Road. For a while, in the present century, the building was used by an eastern food producer. (PPC: Herald Series, M. Peterkin)

Below: Drumchapel Row, a group of workers' homes in East Drumchapel, on the road to Bearsden. A number of children sit at the side of the road to get into the photograph. The brick houses and the housed, then working in this district, are now long gone. A comment on the postcard by a visitor reads: 'This is the Rows; not awfully good I think'. 'Not awfully exaggerated', I think. (PPC: Goldies Series, P.O.)

Opposite below: Garscadden Road, with the entry to Garscadden House on the left, 1912. The village itself is across the field, with a railway track in front of it. Drumchapel was a small place in the country with no near roads wider than that shown for some distance, so the railway was a blessing. The extension of Great Western Road was still many years away. (Valentine 73682, 1912; M. Peterkin)

Above: An Edwardian view of Drumchapel, looking south down Garscadden Road with Drumchapel Road on the left, *c.* 1909. The railway line runs across the view, as today, a short distance down the road, but beyond, nothing much is seen before the Knightswood Rowe is reached. This postcard, from Lewisham sent to the Alderman family in Folkestone, was from Nellie, 'Congratulations, kind wishes and many happy peaceful Years!' (Goldie's Series, P.O. Drumchapel)

Garscadden Road, Drumchapel

GARSCADDEN GATES, DRUMCHAPEL

Garscadden Gates were certainly impressive. When the area was planned for Corporation housing on a big scale, the house became a target too tempting for some of the youngsters to ignore and the gates did not prevent its inevitable destruction in 1959. (PPC: Herald Series; M. Peterkin, P.O.)

Garscadden House, a fairly modest building, with an impressive entrance, *c.* 1912. It was open to the public during the First World War, and apparently to the sender of this postcard to Mme. B. Brain at the Radcliffe Infirmary, Oxford in May 1916. It is likely that Odette, 'Your ever Belgian friend', was an evacuee as well as a friend. (PPC: Valentine 73695; M. Peterkin)

Above: The Western District Rugby Champions in 1909-10 were from the Drumchapel Club. The winning team members are, left to right, back row: G. Allan, J.A. Stewart, A. Sutherland, A. Reid, A.A. Cruickshanks, C.H. Stewart, D.S. Fyle. Middle row: W.S. M'Leod, R. Garroway (Hon. Sec.), R. Cuthbertson (Capt.), F. Hiley, R.M. Drummond. Front: R.H. Rankin, F. Aitken (Hon. Tres.). The man in the cap on the left is not named.

Right: The Peel of Drumry had long survived the Drumry Castle of old and stood till summer 1956 when it was decided by those in charge that it was out of place in such newly erected modern attractive Glasgow housing, in Drumchapel. It took no time at all to disappear. The newly erected housing is seen behind.

Kinfauns Drive enclosed much of the new building above Drumry Road and saw the first modern shopping centre to be built in the area, seen here in 1963. In the early days the new residents welcomed the move from their old cramped, decaying flats with shared lavatories in the city – Drumchapel was a big improvement. (PPC: Valentine D8245)

The Dunkenny Square Shopping Centre when just new on a sunny day in 1963. True-Form, Grant's and Woolworth's were just some of the well-known shops there, with many more on the other side and behind the dividing shelter in front of the view. Unfortunately the coming of the supermarkets took the shine away and it ceased to keep its attractive design. (Valentine D8246)

Opposite below: Linkwood Drive is seen here descending to Kinfauns Drive, not far from the Shopping Centre, after a half-mile course from the east, seen on a snowy morning in February 1956. Rows of new houses are seen here on and beyond Dunkenny Road. The row of houses descending on the right is now gone and Airgold Drive, going off to the right, was also emptied of houses after some time.

THE SHOPPING CENTRE, DRUMCHAPEL, FROM THE EAST

The tall A-shaped sign in the shopping square at Dunkenny displays, vertically, the word 'Centre' and presumably 'Shopping' was on the other side. The building on the right has now been replaced by a greater, if less attractive, one. In the early years transport was a problem for those who moved here and had been used to bus or tram travel with fares no higher than fourpence but these soon rose dramatically. Few at the time had cars and, as with Knightswood, in Corporation-owned areas public houses were forbidden. (Valentine D 8247)

Acknowledgements

Putting together this collection of illustrations, and gathering the information needed to go with them, could not have been done without the help of many friends who have added to my collection and to my knowledge of the area. I have received much willing advice and help.

I admit that while compiling this book I have learned more about the history of my birthplace than ever before. I am sorry for any mistakes that may still be contained here or for anything important that I may have overlooked.

I thank particularly Bill Spalding for his advice, the loan of his pictures of Partick and for checking and correcting of my text. I am also indebted to my brother, John Stewart and to George Waugh and A.J. Douglas for providing photographs, also Bruce Peter for his advice and help with images of the history of the cinema. My gratitude goes to the City Archive at The Mitchell Library, Library of Information and Learning, Glasgow City Council for allowing me to include SRA photographs. The help and advice of Commercial Development Officer, Verina Litster is very much appreciated. St Andrew's University Library gave permission and sought no payment for publication of Valentine pictures and that is greatly appreciated. I thank David Buxton also for his help and advice in producing the book.

Finally, I thank my wife, Margaret, for her help and patience during the time I spent walking the West End and getting it all down on paper.